Mary Pope Osborne

My Favorite Writer

Erinn Banting

WEIGL PUBLISHERS INC.

Published by Weigl Publishers Inc.
350 5th Avenue, Suite 3304, PMB 6G
New York, NY 10118-0069

Web site: www.weigl.com
Copyright ©2007 WEIGL PUBLISHERS INC.

Library of Congress Cataloging-in-Publication Data

Banting, Erinn.
  Mary Pope Osborne / Erinn Banting.
     p. cm. -- (My favorite writer)
  Includes index.
  ISBN 1-59036-482-1 (library binding : alk. paper) -- ISBN 1-59036-
483-X (soft cover : alk. paper)
  1. Osborne, Mary Pope--Juvenile literature. 2. Authors, American--20th
century--Biography--Juvenile literature. 3. Children's stories--
Authorship--Juvenile literature. I. Title. II. Series.
  PS3565.S443Z95 2006
  813'.54--dc22
  [B]

                                                        2006015266

Printed in the United States of America
1 2 3 4 5 6 7 8 9 0 09 08 07 06 05

All of the Internet URLs given in the book were valid at the time of
publication. However, due to the dynamic nature of the Internet, some
addresses may have changed, or sites may have ceased to exist since
publication. While the author and publisher regret any inconvenience this
may cause readers, no responsibility for any such changes can be accepted
by either the author or the publisher.

Project Coordinator
Frances Purslow

Design
Terry Paulhus

Contents

Milestones 5

Early Childhood 6

A Life of Adventure 8

Learning the Craft 12

Getting Published 14

Writer Today 16

Popular Books 18

Creative Writing Tips 22

Writing a Biography Review 24

Fan Information 26

Quiz 28

Writing Terms 30

Glossary 31

Index / Photo Credits 32

Mary Pope Osborne

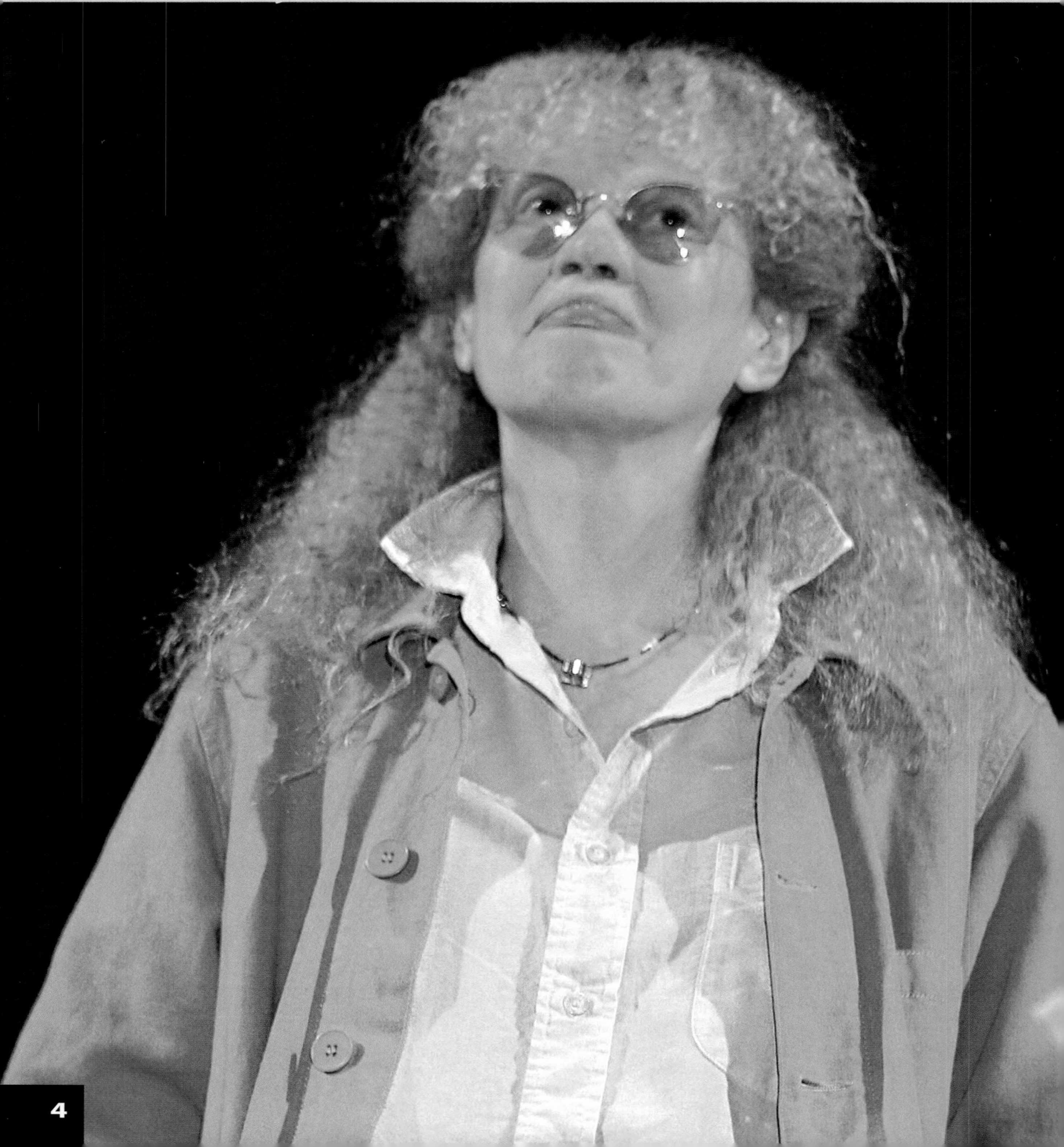

MILESTONES

1949 Born on May 20 in Fort Sill, Oklahoma

1967 Begins college at the University of North Carolina at Chapel Hill

1971 Graduates from college

1972 Travels to Asia

1976 Marries Will Osborne

1982 Publishes her first book, *Run, Run As Fast As You Can*

1992 Publishes the first book in the Magic Tree House series, *Dinosaurs Before Dark*

1993 Is elected the 27th president of the Authors' Guild

2002 The first book from the Tales from the Odyssey series, *The One-Eyed Giant*, is published

2005 Publishes the 34th book in the Magic Tree House series, *Season of the Sandstorms*

2006 *Blizzard of the Blue Moon* is prepared for publication

Mary Pope Osborne's books have been read by millions of children. Before becoming an author, Mary traveled and worked around the world. She began to write books nearly 25 years ago.

The first book in her popular Magic Tree House series was published in the United States in 1992. It was called *Dinosaurs Before Dark*. This book follows the adventures of children Jack and Annie. The two children find a magic tree house filled with books. They soon discover that they can travel to the places described in the books and go on wonderful adventures.

During her career, Mary has written about 80 books. Her books have been translated into more than 15 languages and are enjoyed by children around the world.

Early Childhood

Mary Pope Osborne was born on May 20, 1949, in Fort Sill, Oklahoma. When she was young, Mary and her family traveled a great deal because her father was in the **military**. Before she turned 15 years old, Mary had lived in several parts of the United States and Austria, a country in Europe. Mary moved so many times during her childhood that she formed a close bond with her parents, her twin brother, her younger brother, and her older sister. Because she was so close to her family, Mary never minded moving from place to place.

Mary and her brothers spent much of their time playing and biking in the woods. They liked to pretend they were traveling to far off places and not just climbing trees and splashing in rivers and streams. Mary's imagination enhanced her development as a writer.

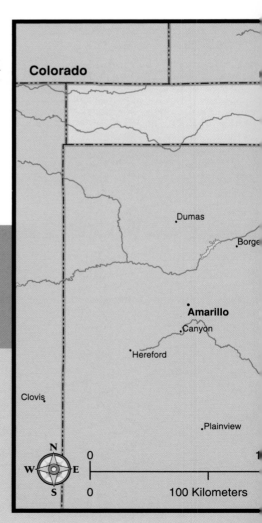

Fort Sill, Oklahoma, is about 85 miles southwest of Oklahoma City. About 12,000 people live in Fort Sill.

Mary craved adventure and travel. When her family finally settled in a small town in North Carolina, Mary was bored. She wished she could see the world. However, she found excitement at a local theater. She worked at the theater as a stage hand and actress. At the theater, Mary could escape the everyday world and be **transported** to different **eras** and places.

Mary's love of the theater, adventure, and travel all helped her later in her life when she was writing books. Many of her stories involve children journeying through time and space. Using their imaginations, Mary and her readers can travel with the characters found in her books.

A Life of Adventure

Mary pursued her love of the theater throughout high school and into college. In 1967, she enrolled in the drama program at the University of North Carolina at Chapel Hill. There she studied acting and theater. In the drama department, Mary leaned how to act, and she also learned about different stories told in theater.

In the drama program, students learned about the history of theater, beginning with the ancient Greeks. The ancient Greeks performed **elaborate** plays in huge **auditoriums**. Many of the plays were about Greek **myths**. These stories remained in Mary's heart and mind. Later, Mary used these stories to inspire her own work.

Greece is home to many old myths and stories that still are told today.

In the early 1970s, Mary **graduated** from college and set off on many adventures. One of her adventures took her on a tour of many countries in Asia. The places she visited included Afghanistan, India, Iraq, Iran, and Pakistan. During this journey, Mary and her companions traveled from place to place in a **caravan**. Mary and her friends camped outdoors, ate food cooked on campfires, bathed in natural bodies of water, and faced other difficult living conditions.

When she was in Kathmandu, a city in Nepal, Mary fell ill. She suffered from blood poisoning, or an infection in her bloodstream. Mary became very sick from the infection and was in the hospital for two weeks. While hospitalized, Mary read The Lord of the Rings, a series of books by J.R.R. Tolkien.

Inspired to Write

In many of Mary's books, her characters face danger and go on exciting adventures. Mary experienced danger many times during her travels: "We traveled through 11 Asian countries and nearly lost our lives, first in an earthquake in northern Afghanistan and then in a riot in Kabul."
Mary Pope Osborne

Once she was well again, Mary returned to the United States. She worked in a number of different jobs in California and Washington, DC. Mary applied her experience as a world traveler when she worked as a travel consultant. Travel consultants help people organize their trips.

Mary had other odd jobs after her illness. She worked in a department store and as a medical assistant. Another exciting development occurred in Mary's life when she moved to Washington. One day, Mary went to see a production at a local theater. It was a **musical** about Jesse James. Jesse was an **outlaw** who led a band of robbers in the mid-1800s.

Mary's interest in history, and the lead actor's white cowboy hat, attracted her to the man playing Jesse. He was Will Osborne. One year later, in 1976, she married Will in New York City.

Mary and her husband, Will, met in Washington, D.C.

In New York City, Mary continued to work odd jobs. She taught acting classes and worked in a restaurant. She also had a job editing for a children's magazine. Mary says that she did not realize it at the time, but this job helped bring her one step closer to her work as an author. As an **editor**, Mary learned what appealed to young people and how to write for them.

Michael Frayn, a British playwright and novelist, is one of Mary's favorite writers.

Favorite Books

Although Mary did not begin to write books until she was older, she has loved to read books since she was a young girl. Mary's favorite book was *Egermeier's Bible Story Book* by Elsie E. Egermeier. Another book Mary loved was *A Little Princess,* by Frances Hodgson Burnett. Mary viewed Sara Crewe, the main character, as a heroine. Mary also loved books by Thomas Wolfe, J.D. Salinger, Virginia Wolfe, Ernest Hemingway, and Vladimir Nabokov. Reading books by these authors inspired Mary to write in different ways. Reading Thomas Wolfe's books, for example, encouraged Mary to use her imagination. Often, children in her stories are put into magical or fantastical situations that are not part of everyday life. Mary still loves to read. Two of her favorite contemporary authors are Ian McEwan and Michael Frayn.

Learning the Craft

"One day, out of the blue, I began writing a story about an 11-year-old girl in the South. The girl was a lot like me, and many of the incidents in the story were similar to happenings in my childhood. ... It became a young adult novel called Run, Run Fast As You Can. Finally I knew what I wanted to be when I grew up."
Mary Pope Osborne

Mary's early childhood, her love of adventure, and the stories and myths she learned in theater school helped her become the author she is today. Her experience as an editor at a children's magazine helped her learn what young people were interested in reading.

Mary's first book, *Run, Run As Fast As You Can,* follows the struggles of an 11-year-old girl named Hallie. Hallie worries about being popular. She also has to face a tragedy after her family moves to Virginia. Mary used her own experiences to help her write the book.

Mary's other books also reflect her personal passions and experiences. Her most popular series, Magic Tree House, began as an idea to write a story about two children who can travel back in time. For nearly a year, Mary thought of ways she could transport her characters through time. She first thought of a museum and an artist's **studio**. Then, on a walk with her husband, Mary came up with the idea of using a magic tree house.

Children enjoy Mary's stories, such as *Night of the New Magicians.*

Her two main characters, Annie and Jack, are quickly whisked away to far off places in time and space. Just by reading one of the books in the tree house and wishing to go to the place in the story, Annie and Jack are able to travel as far away as space and as far back in history as the time of the dinosaurs.

Inspired to Write

"The best part of being a writer is being transported to other places and living other experiences. By surrounding myself with the smells, weather, animals, and people of imaginary landscapes, I feel as if I'm living an extraordinary life. The worst part of being a writer is not having enough time or energy to write all the things I want to write."

Mary Pope Osborne

Mary was inspired to write the Magic Tree House series when she saw a tree house. She knew it was the right vehicle for characters Jack and Annie to travel the world.

Getting Published

"Now 24 years and 80 books later, I think I'm one of the most fortunate people on earth. Whenever I work on a book, I feel as if I've traveled to some amazing place in the world."
Mary Pope Osborne

Mary worked hard to get her first books published. The initial step for any author is to write a first draft. The first draft is the first version of a story. It outlines the action or events of the story and introduces the reader to the characters.

Mary uses experiences or interests from her real life to build her adventures. She says she is a little like the character Jack from the Magic Tree House books. Both she and Jack love to read and learn new things. Mary is also like Annie, another character from the Magic Tree House series. Annie can be **impulsive** and loves animals—just like Mary. However, Mary also says her characters have qualities she does not, such as bravery and quick-thinking skills.

The Publishing Process

Publishing companies receive hundreds of **manuscripts** from authors each year. Only a few manuscripts become books. Publishers must be sure that a manuscript will sell many copies. As a result, publishers reject most of the manuscripts they receive.

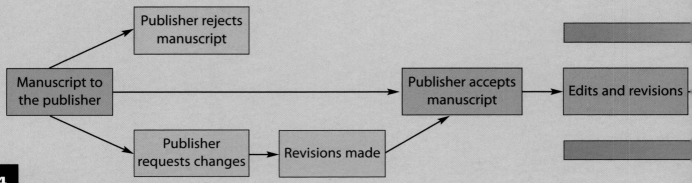

Once Mary completes a first draft, she sends it to an editor. An editor is a person who works for a publishing company. The editor helps authors make **revisions**, or changes to their drafts, so they are ready to print and sell. Mary has worked with the same editor, Mallory Loehr, on all of the books in the Magic Tree House series. Mary says that her books are a result of teamwork with Mallory, who serves as "an inspiration and guide." She also values the support she receives from Sal Murdocca, the illustrator of the Magic Tree House books. Sal's illustrations help bring Mary's fantastic stories to life.

Mary has published more than 35 books in the series, and she continues to write more.

Inspired to Write

Mary does not have a writing routine. Each day is different for her. Sometimes she writes on her laptop computer in the house. On other days, she takes her computer outside when she is ready to work. She also writes at different times during the day.

Once a manuscript has been accepted, it goes through many stages before it is published. Often, authors change their work to follow an editor's suggestions. Once the book is published, some authors receive royalties. This is money based on book sales.

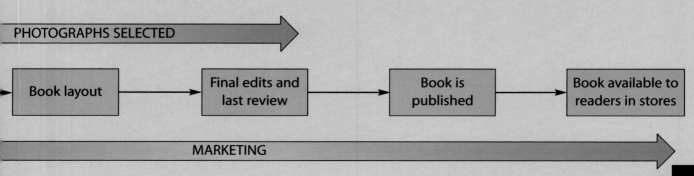

PHOTOGRAPHS SELECTED →

Book layout → Final edits and last review → Book is published → Book available to readers in stores

MARKETING →

Writer Today

Mary Pope Osborne is one of the best-known children's book authors in the world. Readers eagerly await the next book that continues the adventures of Annie and Jack.

Mary gets excited to see how her books turn out, too. She loves to see how the art created for her books goes with the words she has written.

Mary and her husband, Will, split their time between their home in New York City and a cabin in Pennsylvania. Each day when Mary writes, the couple's pet terrier, Bailey, sleeps on top of Mary's desk.

Mary and Will display a scene from Mary's book *Tonight on the Titanic* that was made by a fan.

Mary's Magic Tree House books are among the most popular of her writings. However, she has also published other books and series, in many different **genres**. She has written a mystery series called the Spider Kane Mysteries about a young detective named Spider Kane. Mary's Tales from the Odyssey series tells stories about an ancient figure from Greek mythology named Odysseus. She also writes study guides with her sister that give interested readers more information about the topics covered in her Magic Tree House books.

Along with writing, Mary keeps busy recording audio versions of her books. In her free time, she enjoys staying at her cabin and watching her dogs sniff flowers and swim in the lake.

Mary's book *Blizzard of the Blue Moon* was released in 2006.

Popular Books

M̲ary Pope Osborne has written more than 80 books, including adventure stories, historical fiction, mysteries, and even picture books for younger readers. The following are brief descriptions of some of the most popular books Mary has written.

Dinosaurs Before Dark

One day, Jack and his sister Annie discover a tree house in the forest near their Frog Creek, Pennsylvania, home. When they climb inside, they discover it is filled with books. Little do they know, the books and the tree house are magical. In *Dinosaurs Before Dark,* Jack and Annie discover this exciting secret when Annie picks up a book about dinosaurs. When she wishes she could see a **pteranodon** in real life, Annie is surprised to see one swoop in front of the tree house window.

This begins an exciting adventure in which Jack and Annie travel back in time to an era when dinosaurs ruled Earth.

Midnight on the Moon

In this book, Jack and Annie travel farther than they ever have before. They go all the way to the Moon. Once they arrive at an international space station, they find a set of spacesuits and set out to explore. As they comb the Moon's surface and learn about Earth's fascinating **satellite**, they search for the next in a series of clues given to them by Morgan Le Fay. Morgan is the librarian of Camelot, a mythical land from **medieval** literature. She also controls the Magic Tree House. Morgan has promised the children that if they solve four riddles, she will make them masters of the tree house. In this book, Jack and Annie find their fourth clue.

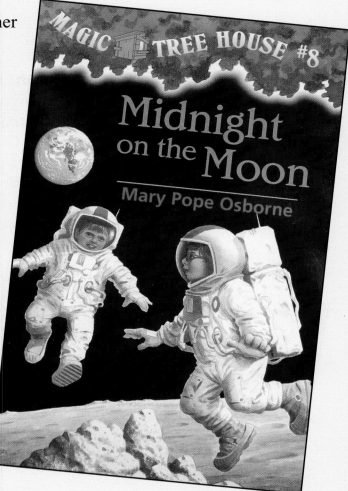

Day of the Dragon King

Jack and Annie find themselves in China in this exciting book. There, they meet an emperor who burns any books he thinks go against his beliefs or the way he rules his **subjects**. In order to get home, Jack and Annie must find a copy of a book containing an ancient Chinese myth. With the help of two friends—a **scholar** and a weaver—they defeat the emperor and find their way home.

Tonight on the Titanic

Jack and Annie find themselves on board the *Titanic* on the very night it is doomed to sink. The *Titanic* was a ship that sank after it hit an iceberg while crossing the Atlantic Ocean. In this exciting book, Jack and Annie must help a brother and sister find their way to a lifeboat so that all four children can be saved.

Stage Fright on a Summer Night

With another clue from Morgan, Jack and Annie make their way back in time to the 1500s. There they find the Globe Theatre. The Globe was famous for holding the first productions of many of Shakespeare's plays. During their adventure, Jack and Annie explore England and even perform in a production of *A Midsummer Night's Dream,* one of Shakespeare's plays.

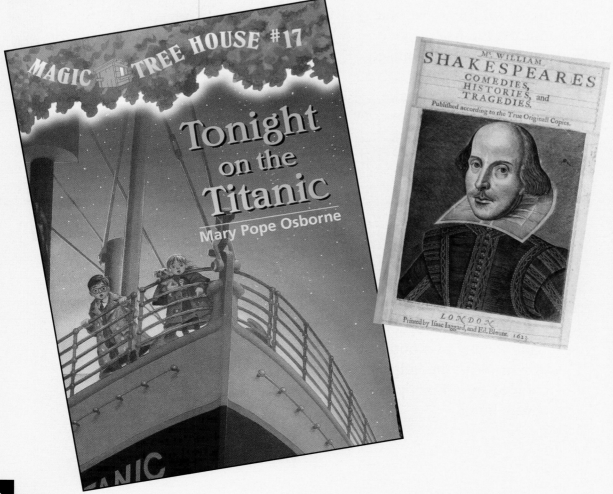

Spider Kane and the Mystery Under the May Apple

Spider Kane is a very smart **arachnid** who finds himself wrapped up in a mystery. Mimi, the girlfriend of his friend Leon Leafwing, is missing. Based on clues from a group of ladybugs, Spider Kane and Leon search for Mimi, encountering many obstacles along the way.

Sirens and Sea Monsters

In this book, Mary Pope Osborne continues the adventures of Odysseus, a brave and strong hero from ancient Greek mythology.

The Odyssey series follows Odysseus' terrifying journey home to Ithaca following the **Trojan War**. On his way home from Troy, where the war was fought, Odysseus and his men meet many obstacles and dangers.

In *Sirens and Sea Monsters,* Odysseus has just returned from the underworld, or Land of the Dead. Odysseus and his men continue to face challenges. Among them is Charybdis, a deadly whirlpool that poses a danger to ships. Those who escape Charybdis still face a challenge from Scylla, a sea monster that tries to trap sailors.

AWARDS
One World, Many Religions

1997 National Council of Teachers of English's Orbis Pictus Honor Award

2005 Educational Paperback Association's Ludington Award for her body of work

Creative Writing Tips

Writing can be a very difficult job, but it can also be very rewarding. Authors such as Mary Pope Osborne work very hard to write books for their fans. A great deal of research goes into every book. Mary also communicates with the fans of her books to find out what they are interested in reading. All writers must practice their craft so that each of their books is better than the last. Here are some tips that might help you be a better writer.

Take Inspiration from Real Life

No one can travel back in time, but many of Mary's characters and stories have been inspired by her real-life adventures. She has even created characters in her books based on her family and her pet dogs. Are there people or stories from your life that you think would make an interesting story? Combine a real situation or person with fictional events.

Mary also uses history in her books. Have you learned about a figure or event in history that you would like to write about? Imagine yourself as a great hero, or being present at a famous event. What do you think it would feel like to be there?

To keep in touch with her fans, Mary attends book signings and writes messages on her website.

Plan an Outline

Now that you have your idea, it is important to write an outline. An outline helps you map out your story. It lists the series of events you want to write about and how you want them to unfold. Before Mary begins writing a book, she refers to each of the characters and each event written in her outline. This helps her stay organized and meet her **deadlines**. Outlines may change, but they are important tools early on to help you plan your story. Start with the events in the story, and then focus on the characters.

Practice

Writing is not just about having a good story and interesting characters. Writers must practice every day to make their writing as good as it can be. Many writers work for years before one of their stories gets published. Take as much time to practice writing as you can each day. It is also important to read as much as you can. Reading helps you learn about other writers and what makes their stories interesting. You can learn a great deal by reading.

Use Your Imagination and Have Fun

Mary's books demonstrate what a vibrant and interesting imagination she has. They also demonstrate her love of history and learning. Mary continues to use her imagination to take her readers to the farthest reaches of time and space. They meet characters, such as Shakespeare, who lived hundreds of years ago. They also journey to places children have never been. Follow Mary's example. Use your imagination, and see where it will take you.

Inspired to Write

"The Magic Tree House has also whisked me to schools all over the country, and the contact I now have with children has brought overwhelming joy into my life. I love the letters I get from them and I love reading countless Magic Tree House stories that they've written. I feel as if these kids and I are all exploring the creative process together, using our imaginations plus our reading and writing skills to take us wherever we want to go. This, I tell my small fellow authors, is true magic."

Mary Pope Osborne

"I've journeyed through Greek mythology, Norse mythology, medieval stories, and American tall tales. I've 'met' George Washington and Ben Franklin, and without even leaving my home, I've traveled around the globe, learning about the religions of the world."
Mary Pope Osborne

Writing a Biography Review

A biography is an account of an individual's life that is written by another person. Some people's lives are very interesting. In school, you may be asked to write a biography review. The first thing to do when writing a biography review is to decide whom you would like to learn about. Your school library or community library will have a large selection of biographies from which to choose.

Are you interested in an author, a sports figure, an inventor, a movie star, or a president? Finding the right book is your first task. Whether you choose to write your review on a biography of Mary Pope Osborne or another person, the task will be similar.

Begin your review by writing the title of the book, the author, and the person featured in the book. Then, start writing about the main events in the person's life. Include such things as where the person grew up and what his or her childhood was like. You will want to add details about the person's adult life, such as whether he or she married or had children. Next, write about what you think makes this person special. What kinds of experiences influenced this individual? For instance, did he or she grow up in unusual circumstances? Was the person determined to accomplish a goal? Include any details that surprised you. A concept web is a useful research tool. Use the concept web on the right to begin researching your biography review.

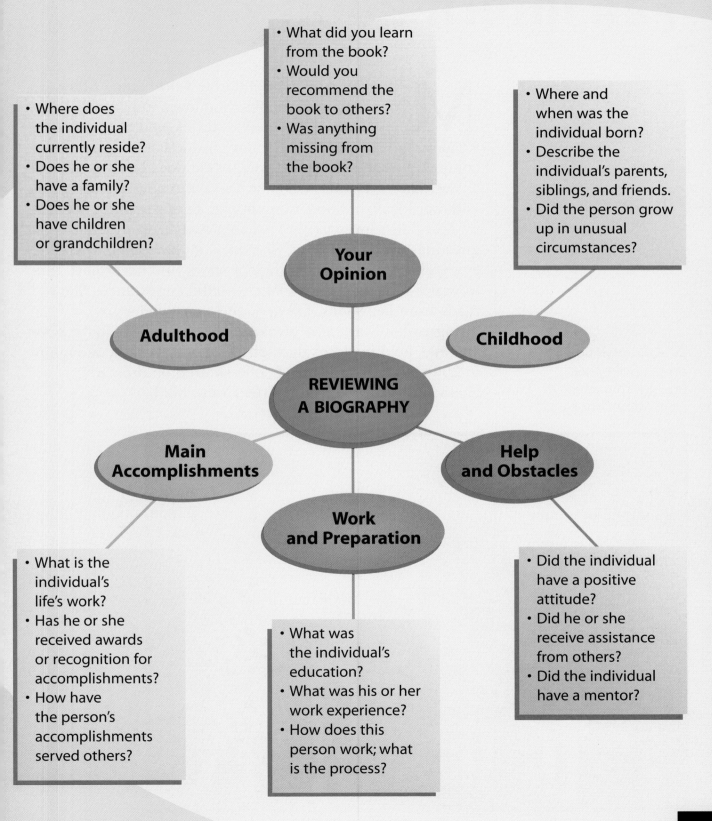

- Where does the individual currently reside?
- Does he or she have a family?
- Does he or she have children or grandchildren?

- What did you learn from the book?
- Would you recommend the book to others?
- Was anything missing from the book?

- Where and when was the individual born?
- Describe the individual's parents, siblings, and friends.
- Did the person grow up in unusual circumstances?

Your Opinion

Adulthood

Childhood

REVIEWING A BIOGRAPHY

Main Accomplishments

Help and Obstacles

Work and Preparation

- What is the individual's life's work?
- Has he or she received awards or recognition for accomplishments?
- How have the person's accomplishments served others?

- What was the individual's education?
- What was his or her work experience?
- How does this person work; what is the process?

- Did the individual have a positive attitude?
- Did he or she receive assistance from others?
- Did the individual have a mentor?

Fan Information

illions of readers around the world enjoy Mary Pope Osborne's books. She loves to hear what they think of her books, stories, and characters. Readers can send Mary letters or questions through the companies that publish her books. She does her best to answer each question, whether it is about how she comes up with her ideas, her upcoming books, or her favorite books.

Mary also loves to visit her fans and answer their questions about her work. She does not have time to visit every city where her fans live, or she would never have time to write. When she does make a public appearance, Mary reads from her books, answers questions, and signs **autographs**. Mary also gives autographs to her fans at book signings held in stores that sell her works. At a book signing in 2006, readers in Pennsylvania showed up dressed as characters from the Magic Tree House books.

Fans sometimes dress up like their favorite characters from Mary's books.

The Internet has many websites dedicated to Mary Pope Osborne, her books, and her characters. These sites have been created by publishers and even Mary herself. Other sites have been created by fans who want to share information and their thoughts about Mary's books. There are also many sites that include interviews with Mary and questions from her fans that she has answered.

Mary attends book signings where she can meet her fans.

WEB LINKS

Mary Pope Osborne's Official Website
www.marypopeosborne.com

Visitors to Mary Pope Osborne's website can read information on her past books, projects she is working on, and even her family and pets. This site also has a newsletter that gives readers updated information on a regular basis.

The Official Magic Tree House Website
www.randomhouse.com/kids/magictreehouse

Visitors to the Magic Tree House website can read information about the books and characters in the series. The site also contains information on Mary Pope Osborne, activities, and news. In addition, fans can join the Readers and Writers Club, which teaches them about books and writing.

Quiz

Q: Where and when was Mary Pope Osborne born?

A: Fort Sill

Q: What was the name of Mary's first book?

A: Run, Run As Fast As You Can

Q: What are the names of the main characters in Mary's Magic Tree House Series?

A: Jack and Annie

4

Q: What did Mary's father do for a living?

A: He worked in the military.

5

Q: Where did Mary go to college?

A: The University of North Carolina at Chapel Hill

6

Q: Which of Mary's early jobs helped her learn what young people liked to read?

A: Her job as an editor for a children's magazine

7

Q: What illness did Mary suffer from in Kathmandu?

A: Blood poisoning

8

Q: What are some of the series of books Mary has written?

A: The Spider Kane Mysteries, Tales from the Odyssey series, and the Magic Tree House series

9

Q: Before writing a story or a book, what should you do?

A: Write an outline.

10

Q: Approximately how many books has Mary written?

A: Mary has written about 80 books.

Writing Terms

This glossary will introduce you to some of the main terms in the field of writing. Understanding these common writing terms will allow you to discuss your ideas about books and writing with others.

action: the moving events of a work of fiction

antagonist: the person in the story who opposes the main character

autobiography: a history of a person's life written by that person

biography: a written account of another person's life

character: a person in a story, poem, or play

climax: the most exciting moment or turning point in a story

episode: a short piece of action, or scene, in a story

fiction: stories about characters and events that are not real

foreshadow: hinting at something that is going to happen later in the book

imagery: a written description of a thing or idea that brings an image to mind

narrator: the speaker of the story who relates the events

nonfiction: writing that deals with real people and events

novel: published writing of considerable length that portrays characters within a story

plot: the order of events in a work of fiction

protagonist: the leading character of a story; often a likable character

resolution: the end of the story, when the conflict is settled

scene: a single episode in a story

setting: the place and time in which a work of fiction occurs

theme: an idea that runs throughout a work of fiction

Glossary

arachnid: the class of creatures that includes spiders

auditoriums: buildings where performances are held

autographs: a signature from a person who is well-known or famous

caravan: a procession of vehicles that travel together

deadlines: the dates when something is due

editor: a person who helps a writer revise his or her work before it is published

elaborate: complicated and detailed

eras: periods in history

genres: specific types or kinds of literature

graduated: completed a course of study or degree

impulsive: acting quickly, often without thinking

manuscripts: drafts of a story before it is published

medieval: something from the period of history between 500 and 1450

military: to do with soldiers or the armed forces

musical: a play set to music

myths: traditional stories, accepted as history

outlaw: a person who is wanted by the law

pteranodon: a winged dinosaur

revisions: changes

satellite: an object that revolves around another object

scholar: someone who studies and is an expert in a particular subject

studio: a place where an artist works

subjects: people who live under the authority of a king or queen

transported: moved from one place to another

Trojan War: a war in which ancient Greece defeated the city of Troy

Index

Asia 5, 9

Blizzard of the Blue Moon 5, 17
blood poisoning 9, 29

Day of the Dragon King 19
Dinosaurs Before Dark 5, 18

Fort Sill 5, 6, 28

Greek myths 8, 12, 21, 23, 29

The Lord of the Rings 9

Magic Tree House 5, 12, 14, 15, 16, 17, 18, 19, 20, 23, 28, 29
Midnight on the Moon 19

New York City 10, 11, 16

Osborne, Will 5, 10

Run, Run as Fast as You Can 5, 12, 28

Spider Kane 17, 21, 29
Stage Fright on a Summer Night 20

Tales from the Odyssey 5, 21
theater 6, 7, 8, 10, 12
Tonight on the Titanic 16, 20, 21

University of North Carolina 5, 8, 29

Washington 10

Photo Credits

Every reasonable effort has been made to trace ownership and to obtain permission to reprint copyright material. The publishers would be pleased to have any errors or omissions brought to their attention so that they may be corrected in subsequent printings.

Little Look and Find™

Disney · PIXAR
FINDING NEMO

Illustrated by Art Mawhinney
Cover illustration by
the Disney Storybook Artists

Published by Louis Weber, C.E.O., Publications International, Ltd.
7373 North Cicero Avenue, Lincolnwood, Illinois 60712

Ground Floor, 59 Gloucester Place, London W1U 8JJ

Customer Service: 1-800-595-8484 or
customer_service@pilbooks.com

www.pilbooks.com

p i kids is a registered trademark of Publications International, Ltd.
Look and Find is a registered trademark of Publications International, Ltd.,
in the United States and in Canada.
Little Look and Find is a trademark of Publications International, Ltd.

8 7 6 5 4 3 2 1

ISBN-13: 978-1-4127-6516-9
ISBN-10: 1-4127-6516-1

pi
kids®
publications international, ltd.

Today is Nemo's first day of school. He and his father Marlin meet the teacher, Mr. Ray, at the schoolyard. Oh no, Nemo has wandered off with some of his classmates! Can you locate Nemo, his new school chums, their parents, and Mr. Ray in all this hustle and bustle?

Nemo

Pearl

Ted

Phil

Bob

Sheldon

Tad

Mr. Ray

Nemo wanders too far away and is captured by a human diver! Marlin and his new friend, Dory, go into dangerous waters to look for clues that will help them find Nemo. Keep an eye out for these dangerous-looking sharks skulking about in the underwater minefield. Will Marlin and Dory make it through safely?

Chum

Bruce

Anchor

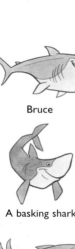

A basking shark

A whale shark

A sand shark

A tiger shark

Nemo is placed into a fish tank. As it turns out, the diver who caught him is actually a dentist who loves fish! But life in an aquarium is not much fun. Help Nemo and the other fish in the tank pass the time by finding all these things in the dentist's waiting room:

Dentists' Daily newspaper

A tooth mug

A fish painting

Swedish fish

Fish crackers

A fish lunch box

A rainbow fish

There is an address on a diver's mask Marlin and Dory find near the sub: "P. Sherman, 42 Wallaby Way, Sydney." But how will they get there when they can barely read? Some helpful moonfish make quite an "impression" by pointing the pair in the right direction. Can you help Marlin and Dory spot these other impressive moonfish signs?

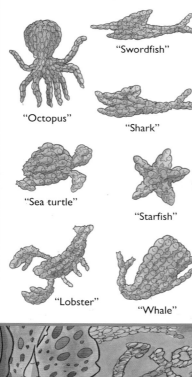

"Swordfish"

"Octopus"

"Shark"

"Sea turtle"

"Starfish"

"Lobster"

"Whale"

Marlin and Dory take a wrong turn, and now they're in the middle of a giant forest of jellyfish! Using your finger, trace the way out without touching any of their stinging tentacles. *Ouch!*

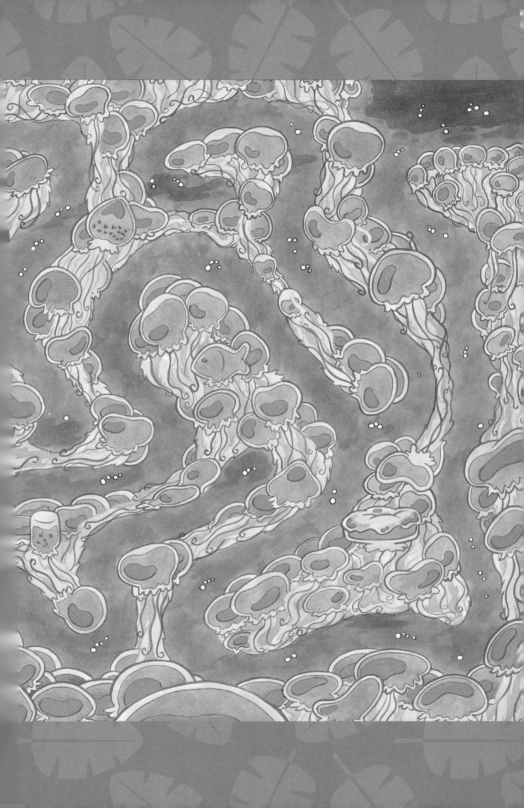

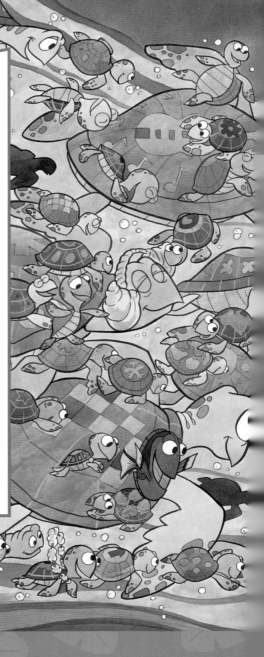

Whoa! After escaping the jellyfish forest, Marlin and Dory meet up with a group of friendly turtles, including Crush and his son Squirt. They're all cruising down the East Australian Current, which should drop them off right by Sydney! See if you can scope out Crush, Squirt, and these other gnarly, shelled dudes!

Squirt

Crush

Flora

Checkers

Noelle

Target

Sydney

Pelé

Once they get to Sydney, a nice pelican named Nigel takes Marlin and Dory to the dentist's office — just as Nemo and his new aquarium friends stage a daring escape! Gill, the leader of the Tank Gang, helps Nemo make his way to the spit sink, because "all drains lead to the ocean." As he flips and flops his way to safety, look around for all these other toothy things!

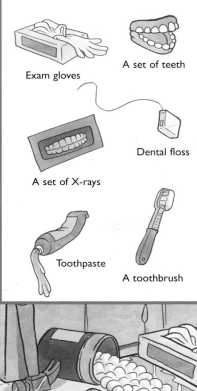

Exam gloves

A set of teeth

A set of X-rays

Dental floss

Toothpaste

A toothbrush

Back in the ocean, Marlin and Nemo are reunited at last—but the excitement is not over yet! The two clown fish help a netful of fish pull off an escape of their own from some local fishermen. Now the grateful groupers are showering the pair with thanks! Can you find Marlin, Nemo, and these other fish in this seaworthy celebration?

Marlin

Nemo

This grouper

Dory

This grouper

This grouper

Peach, the starfish, gets really bored with her face up against the tank glass all day. Can you count how many of these things she can see in the dentist's waiting room?

____ flowers on the wallpaper
____ stuffed animals
____ seashells
____ toothbrushes
____ cans of fish food

Swim on back to the reef to find these school-related things:

❏ jar of squid ink
❏ stones in the shape of pluses and minuses
❏ seaweed macrame
❏ algae map of Australia

Those helpful moonfish have even more great impressions than the ones they showed Marlin and Dory. Can you find these, too?

❏ "anchor"
❏ "sailboat"
❏ "diver"
❏ "arrow"
❏ "pirate flag"
❏ "life preserver"

Go back to the submarine with Bruce and his vegetarian friends. Over the years, many divers have tried to explore the sunken sub, but for some reason they can't get out of there fast enough! Can you spot the things the divers left behind?

❏ diver's fin
❏ diver's mask
❏ underwater flashlight
❏ weight belt
❏ scuba tank
❏ underwater camera

Go back to the jellyfish forest. If you look closely, some of the jellies look different from the rest. Can you spot these strangely familiar jellyfish?

❏ a moon jelly
❏ a jelly fish
❏ a jelly roll
❏ a peanut-butter-and-jellyfish
❏ a jelly mold
❏ a strawberry jelly

Go back and visit Crush, Squirt, and the rest of the sea turtles. Can you find these other distinctive shell patterns on some of the sea turtles riding the East Australian Current?

- ❏ a map of Australia
- ❏ a sand dollar
- ❏ a spider web
- ❏ a hopscotch board
- ❏ a palm tree

Not long after Nemo escapes, it seems the rest of the Tank Gang make their way to freedom, as well! Turn back a page and try to find them as they swim back into the Big Blue.

Gill

Jacques

Peach

Bloat

Gurgle

The dentist likes to spoil his bratty little niece, Darla. Go back to the dentist's office and try to find these presents he bought for her birthday:

- ❏ a doll
- ❏ a beach ball
- ❏ a baton
- ❏ a box of socks
- ❏ a pair of roller skates

Deb (and Flo)

Bubbles